Shadows of the
GREAT WESTERN

R. J. BLENKINSOP

Published by:
Oxford Publishing Co.
5 Lewis Close
Risinghurst
Oxford

PREFACE

The title for this book of photographs has presented a problem, as my collection was started after the 1948 Nationalisation, but portrays a subject which continued for a number of years as if it were still the G.W.R. Today there is tremendous interest in those locomotives and rolling stock which were taken into British Railways Western Region nearly a quarter of a century ago. There is a variety of books on the subject of the Great Western and from time to time reasons are put forward why it is the favourite of the grouping companies. My own feeling is that with a standard range of engines developed over many years, finished to a high standard of workmanship, together with a magnificent display of copper and brass, they appealed to the railway enthusiast on vision alone. My first awakening to what was the G.W.R. was being pushed in my pram along the footpath at Priory Pool in Warwick where above the embankment could be seen the top of the engines as they flashed by on their way to London.

This interest in "watching the trains go by" lay dormant until after the war when at school I used to watch "The Bournemouth Belle" speed through Winchester just after lunch behind a well groomed "Merchant Navy Pacific".

A camera became the way of recording the steam train as even in those days I realised that some form of motive power was bound to replace steam, although at the time I was not sure what form it would take.

Living near Leamington Spa influenced where my camera should point and, in selecting pictures for this book, it is inevitable that many are taken nearby. At the time I was taking these photographs—holidays, weekends and summer evenings—I hardly considered that one day they would be published.

My approach to Railway photographs, whilst influenced by the work of others, is definitely "middle of the road" and the locomotive and train must be the prime consideration. If the surroundings allow for a pleasant view of the country or atmosphere of the station, so much the better.

It is the emotional effect of the steam locomotive which I try to portray in all its various moods and personalities. How difficult it is to put this over in words to someone who does not possess this feeling deep down inside.

Probably anyone reading this preface will have the "something" and will recall the thrill as the minutes drag slowly by waiting for a particular train to appear.

Imagine being out in the country one spring day visiting the Worcester line, say in 1953. The excitement building up during the final fifteen minutes waiting for the up mid-morning train from Worcester is intense.
Would the down train pass and ruin the picture?
Would the engine be clean?
Would it produce smoke?
Would there be sunshine?
As the signal comes off with a crash she must be through Honeybourne running to time—audible now—look up at the sky to see if the sun will be out—check exposure setting—load shutter—now she is in view coming round the curve—magnificent sight, polished green and black paint, burnished copper and brass—how those cleaners must have worked all morning down at Worcester shed—wait until the smokebox obscures the bush on the other side of the line and then press the button.
Immediately one can relax, wave to the driver, see the fireman hard at work, and as the coaches go by into Campden Tunnel look at the passengers in the nearby window reading, sleeping or having a sumptuous lunch in the dining car.
The final coach disappears into the tunnel, the smoke wafts away into the trees and the sun goes in behind a black cloud. Peace descends on the surroundings, the emotional experience is over and one summons up enough strength to go through it all again.
At the end of the day there may be two or three rolls taken or possibly only one or two shots depending on the circumstances. But the activity is not yet over as I must hurry home to develop the negatives and check for quality before hanging up to dry for the night.
I must have carried out this procedure hundreds of times but alas no more after August 1968 when steam disappeared from British Rail.
This book portrays some of the three thousand photographs I have taken between 1951 and the end of 1956. It is a small sample of what I have available but many are not suitable for publication or cover the other regions of British Rail for which I have **equal** affection.
I believe it **was** worth all the effort to produce this book and hope you, the reader, can relive what it was like in steam days—if there is sufficient demand we can continue the story until the end of steam on the former Great Western Railway.

No. 7017 **G. J. Churchward** has just emerged from Whiteball Tunnel and starts the run to Exeter with the down "Torbay Express".

Fitted with the old pattern tall chimney No. 5070 **Sir Daniel Gooch** blackens the sky as it hauls the 13-coach 11.10 Paddington-Birkenhead up Hatton Bank on a dull day. The freight loop from Budbrooke to Hatton station is on the right and notice the telephone box for the banker to inform Hatton Signal box of its arrival.   **12 January 1952**

The L.N.W.R. signals at Leamington Avenue station always dominated the skyline when taking photographs from the east end of the G.W.R. station. There No. 7218 2-8-2T sets off from the up goods loop with a coal train for Banbury. The signals at the end of the up platform are unusual as they control two lines. Normal G.W.R. practice is for each line to have its own signal post.   **21 October 1951**

My photographic activities started just in time to see the last of the Star Class operating. No. 4021 **British Monarch** with elbow steam pipes, runs into Leamington with a Sunday semi-fast from Birmingham to Oxford.   **21 October 1951**

Harbury Cutting is some 6 miles south of Leamington and up trains were clearly audible climbing past Fosse Box sometime before rounding the curve at the start of the cutting. No. 6006 **King George I** in blue livery passes on the 11.35 Wolverhampton to Paddington. The first coach is a 1908 "Concertina" Brake third.　　　　　　　　　　**19 January 1952**

The top end of Harbury cutting runs into Southern Road and Harbury Station and an up freight is passing the signal box behind 2-8-2T No. 7251. There is another freight in the up loop waiting to follow on its way south. Notice the typical Great Western signal box with blue brick base and metal chimney for the signalman's stove.　　　**19 January 1952**

The land near Harbury Cement works was often covered in cement dust blown out by the chimney in the picture. No. 6011 **King James I** is at the head of the 0900 Birmingham-Paddington. On cold days pictures were often marred by steam leaking from the inside cylinders of the 4-cylinder engines.　　　　　　　　　　**9 February 1952**

"A" shop in Swindon works dull and cold on a winter Sunday morning. **North Star** can be seen on its plinth in the background with four Kings and one Castle in various stages of repair. Note the clean and orderly condition of the workshop—no bits and pieces lying about. The locomotive transverser would run across the picture in the foreground.

17 January 1952

Just two days after it hauled the funeral train of King George VI from Paddington to Windsor, No. 4082 **Windsor Castle** stands in Swindon Works with the Royal Coat of Arms hidden under a cover on the side of the smoke box.

The engine is in fact No. 7013 **Bristol Castle** which became **Windsor Castle** after changing over the name and number plates together with the brass plate on the cabside commemorating the visit of King George V to Swindon Works in 1924 when he drove the engine.

The reason for the name change was because the original **Windsor Castle** was awaiting a major overhaul and therefore not in acceptable condition.   **17 January 1952**

Two pictures of No. 6004 **King George III** on the 11.35 Wolverhampton-Paddington. On the right near Bishops Itchington on 23 February 1952 and below in immaculate blue livery approaching the short tunnel in Harbury Cutting, on 22 March 1952.

The driver takes a rest at Gloucester station as No. 2920 **Saint David** awaits the return of passengers from Gloucester shed. Organised by the Midland area of the Stephenson Locomotive Society this was as usual a most interesting run calling at Gloucester, Swindon and Banbury. The engine is in black livery lined out in cream and red with red background to the nameplate.
15 June 1952

Saint David climbs Sapperton Bank and into the tunnel at the summit. Next to the down line can be seen a banner repeater signal required on a falling gradient where with sharp curves a driver required advanced notice of the main signal further down the line. There is also a permanent way slack indicator standing on its own wooden tripod.
15 June 1952

Outside Swindon running shed Ex-works No. 6026 **King John** produces the pungent smell much appreciated by the steam enthusiast. The cover for one of the boiler wash out plugs near the top of the firebox needs clamping in position. The fixings for securing the boiler to the frames, and, at the same time allowing for expansion, are clearly visible in front of the rear splasher. **15 June 1952**

Gloucester shed with 0-4-2T No. 1413, displaying its pre-nationalisation livery. Fitted for auto-coach working, the recessed footsteps are also shown to comply with the loading of gauge. **Saint David** is seen in the background. **15 June 1952**

R.O.D. No. 3023 awaits its turn to be run in after a major overhaul. Always a difficult place for photographs in the afternoon as the sun shines from behind the engines. These 2-8-0's built at Gorton to Robinson design have such Swindon features as cab fittings, buffers, and numberplate with G.W.R. above the number, signifying that it was an absorbed engine. **15 June 1952**

A study in power at rest No. 7034 **Ince Castle** having completed "Running In" awaits its return to Bristol (Bath Road) shed for top link work. A fire rake rests in the foreground and the shed chimneys are visible which were originally made from wooden planks. **15 June 1952**

Inside the stock shed at Swindon are a row of Midland and South Western Junction railway 2-4-0's Nos. 1334/5/6. The gas lighting in the roof above the chimney of 1335 shows the operating valve controlled by pulling the circular hook for "on" or the diamond hook for "off".   **15 June 1952**

This is a general view outside Swindon shed and shows typical atmospheric pollution so much adored by lovers of the steam engine. Among engines on view are:—

No. 6828   **Trellech Grange**
No. 5016   **Montgomery Castle**
No. 6026   **King John**
No. 4062   **Malmesbury Abbey**

A variety of chimney shapes may be studied in this picture.   **15 June 1952**

The Stephenson Locomotive Society ran a special train to Shipston on Stour behind M.S.W.J.R. 2-4-0 No. 1335 (**Above**) the train returns from Shipston on its way back to Moreton in Marsh and is shown crossing the Fosse Way. The four-way bull's eye lamp should be noted on the gate, informing both train and road user how the gates are set. Two red and two white lights are incorporated in the lamp.   **31 August 1952**

Approaching Longdon Road on its way to Shipston. It was here that the Shipston branch left the original Stratford to Moreton tramway.
                                                        31 August 1952

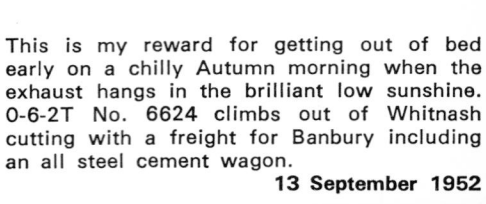

0-6-0 PT No. 5408 has just crossed the now demolished Severn Bridge. Built in 1932 it was the first of the class to be withdrawn in 1956. The 5400 class had 5′ 2″ diameter wheels and were auto fitted, designed for light passenger work. Note the L.M.S. station nameboard and Midland fencing.

12 July 1952

The typical state of cleanliness achieved by Cardiff Canton shed on No. 5020 **Trematon Castle** as it runs along beside the Thames near Pangbourne. Note that even the top part of the copper chimney has been polished. ''The Red Dragon'' arrived in Paddington three hours after leaving Cardiff at 10.00.

5 July 1952

This is my reward for getting out of bed early on a chilly Autumn morning when the exhaust hangs in the brilliant low sunshine. 0-6-2T No. 6624 climbs out of Whitnash cutting with a freight for Banbury including an all steel cement wagon.

13 September 1952

Working home to Chester with the Margate-Birkenhead through train. No. 1022 **County of Northampton** awaits the signals at Oxford. The L.N.W.R. shed is in the background. Above the engine are backing signals with indicator boards and the engineman is crossing the bridge over "Duke's Cut" connecting the River Cherwell with the Thames.   **4 October 1952**

No. 4943 **Marrington Hall** accelerates away from Hatton North Junction with a down freight.
11 October 1952

Steam shut off and the fireman peering round the side of the cab waiting to see the distant signal for Fosse Box, 2-8-0 No. 2814 rattles out of the short tunnel in Harbury Cutting.   **8 March 1953**

Seen working a Birmingham-Oxford semi-fast, No. 4053 **Princess Alexandra** hurries by near Warwick power station with the driver seated in the usual rather uncomfortable position. The brass beading on the splashers of the Stars was removed during the first world war.   **28 February 1953**

It must happen by the law of averages that if you lean over a bridge enough times two trains will appear together. Here 2-6-2T No. 5152 is in charge of a Leamington-Birmingham local while No. 5185 assists a freight up the slow line on Hatton Bank.
28 February 1953

A view which I seldom bothered to photograph—the branch line train arriving at the main line station. In this case it is 0-4-2T No. 1444 at Cholsey and Moulsford coming in from Wallingford, with one of the later type Auto-coaches. There is a wealth of material in this photograph for the railway modeller.

A few hundred yards south of the station, the line runs into a deep chalk cutting crossed by a handsome brick bridge for the use of the local farmer. No 4053 **Princess Alexandra** comes up the grade with a London-Wolverhampton express via Oxford.   **7 April 1953**

Another view at Cholsey and Moulsford showing an up freight passing through on the slow line behind 2-6-2T No. 6100. The first of the class built in 1931 for working the London suburban services and rarely used on goods turns, was also the first of the class to be withdrawn in 1958.   **7 April 1953**

This is one of my favourite locations where the line is climbing out of Leamington and emerges from a cutting to run on an embankment all the way up to Harbury Cutting. No. 6013 **King Henry VIII** accelerates the 18.00 Birmingham-Paddington up the bank with a generous exhaust.

23 April 1953

Coming down through Harbury Cutting at speed in a typical early spring scene before the leaves are showing. No. 5055 **Earl of Eldon** has the morning Paddington-Birmingham via Oxford. This was a maddening train as on a number of occasions it passed as the 12.00 Birmingham-Paddington was coming the other way. For a near miss you can see the last coach disappearing on the down line of the earlier picture of No. 6004 taken on 22 March 1952.

22 March 1953

Shrub Hill station Worcester where No. 2920 **Saint David** has just uncoupled from a Hereford-Worcester train which after strengthening will go on to London behind No. 5993 **Kirby Hall**. Note the recess in the down platform to allow clearance when the scissor crossing is used. Direct design descent can be seen in comparing the Hall with the Saint. **6 June 1953**

Another Stephenson Locomotive Society outing to Swindon which took in the M.S.W.J.R. down to Andover and back via Basingstoke and Reading. Dukedog 4-4-0 No. 9000 takes water at Cheltenham Landsdown while the passengers take fresh air and photographs. Note the stately glass awning over the platforms. **14 June 1953**

At Andover Q.I. 0-6-0 No. 33022 runs by with "The Lolly Man" chalked on the front of the smokebox. Mr. W. A. Camwell, who organised these specials and who is the Editor of the S.L.S. Journal, stands by the Buffer Beam of No. 9000.　　**14 June 1953**

0-6-0 Pannier tank No. 1991 of the 850 class and Taff Vale railway 0-6-2T No. 309 outside Swindon stock shed. A Dukedog can also be seen. On the pannier tank you will notice the square wheel spokes, buffer beam above the running plate, and the panelled splashers.　　**14 June 1953**

This makes an interesting study for the model maker and shows the 6-wheel bogie of W. 9001 standing in the down bay at Leamington after conveying American Railroad officials for a tour of the Shakespeare

The A.T.C. ramp is visible on the right and detonators are in position for the up fast in Leamington station. No. 6011 **King James I** awaits the

variety of coaching stock make up the 10.15 Paddington-Wolverhampton as it leaves Leamington behind No. 5960 **Saint Edmund Hall** in polished black livery, a credit to the cleaners at Oxford shed. A G.W.R. railcar is in the bay and a wagon used for carrying aircraft propellers is on the left with the Avenue station behind.
19 September 1953

On a foggy morning No. 1004 **County of Somerset** heads the "Cornishman" Wolverhampton-Penzance out of Gloucester Eastgate station. Un-rebuilt Patriot No. 45509 **The Derbyshire Yeomanry** waits with a train from Birmingham New Street to Bristol.
18 November 1953

At Leamington with blower on and awaiting the "right away" No. 5032 **Usk Castle** has Hatton Bank ahead to climb with the 11.10 Paddington-Birkenhead. **16 November 1953**

photography where it was cold and the exhaust helps to make a live picture. No. 5027 **Farleigh Castle** makes a fine sight with the 11.10 Paddington-Birkenhead as part of the fireman's efforts goes straight up the chimney. The leading coach is the only example of 70′ top light brake third with 6-wheel bogies. Note that the track was about to be relayed and on the left is a fogman's hut. **28 November 1953**

Wrong line working on a Sunday morning with 0-6-2T No. 6697 (now preserved) in the foreground and No. 6879 **Overton Grange** passing on a freight to Birmingham. The location is between Warwick and Leamington where the line is crossed by the Grand Union Canal seen in the background with another 0-6-2T underneath. **14 February 1954**

2-6-2T No. 5185 hurries down Hatton Bank with a local from Birmingham to Leamington. **7 March 1954**

A well built example of a loading gauge stands on the right of the picture as 2-6-2T No. 6130 picks up speed after the Shrivenham stop with a Reading-Swindon train. **6 March 1954**

Perhaps not looking as clean as it does today but nevertheless a credit to the cleaners at Stafford Road shed, No. 4079 **Pendennis Castle** climbs out of Leamington with the up "Inter-City". The early pattern of inside cylinder covers show up well in this picture.

Halls at Speed
No. 4956 **Plowden Hall** with an up train and No. 6998 **Burton Agnes Hall** (now preserved) forging westwards into the evening sun, both taken from the same spot two miles east of Didcot. In the top photograph the fireman can be seen hard at work and the water scoop is prominent under the tender.
19 April 1954

Cup Final Day sometimes produced a succession of football specials to Wembley depending on who were the lucky participants. No doubt soccer enthusiasts can work out which supporters were being hauled by No. 6862 **Derwent Grange** as it comes up the divided main line near Saunderton with a special from Birmingham to Wembley. The cheery crew must have spotted me some way away as the driver has come over to the fireman's side of the engine.
1 May 1954

"It's the one with the bell" was the usual cry from the engine spotters on the bridge in the background whenever No. 6000 **King George V** came into sight at the end of Whitnash cutting. Here it is working the 18.00 Birmingham-Paddington. **19 July 1954**

0-4-2T No. 1402 propels 70' Auto-coach No. W206 into Honeybourne station from the Cheltenham line. The coach is gas lit with the gas pipes on top of the roof. Originally it was railmotor No. 86 but converted in 1933. **7 August 1954**

Under a stormy sky No. 6009 **King Charles II** approaches Hatton station with the 15.00 Birmingham-Paddington express. The Grand Union Canal is seen above the hedge on the right and the tracks to the left are for Stratford-upon-Avon and the south west. **11 August 1954**

picture taken than watching 2-6-0 No. 5395 take the 7-coach down "Cambrian Coast Express" out of Shrewsbury station with another load of holidaymakers. Note the automatic train control pick-up under the buffer beam and the two platelayers in earnest conversation standing in the middle of the down main line having left their hammer beside the track.

12 August 1954

My first visit to "Glorious Devon" was damp to say the least but when sights such as this came into view it did not matter too much. Approaching Aller Junction with a train to Plymouth is No. 7815 **Fritwell Manor** with 2-6-2T No. 5150 on the inside. In the background a local train approaches for the Torquay line.

21 August 1954

2-6-2T No. 4179 at Aller Junction is on the down line for Torquay and No. 5024 **Carew Castle** comes off the branch with a Kingswear-Wolverhampton train. The rivets on the side of the tank engine's bunker clearly show the space allocated to coal and water. **21 August 1954**

Cowley Bridge Junction looking north with the Southern line from Barnstable coming in on the left. 2-8-0 No. 3838 approaches Exeter and according to the signals is about to cross over the main line. Note the long check rails and point rodding outside the signal box where under the steps can be seen a goodly store of locomotive coal for the signal-

2-6-0 No. 6398 pulls away from Tiverton Junction with an evening local train from Taunton to Exeter. The branch to Hemyock leaves beyond the station and disappears through the trees above the goods yard. There is plenty to interest the railway modeller in this picture.

23 August 1954

No. 6018 **King Henry VI** bursts out of the tunnel at the start of the promenade at Dawlish with the 08.30 Plymouth-Paddington. The leading coach is "Centenary Stock" built in 1935 to mark the centenary of the G.W.R. A sighting board helps the engineman on the down line to read the signal arm against the distracting background.

25 August 1954

At the other end of the tunnel shown on the preceding page, No. 4942 **Maindy Hall** emerges with a local train from Exeter, and 2-8-0 No. 2845 has the up line. The seashore beach huts are visible on the right of the picture. **25 August 1954**

A seven coach train with a history of coaching stock. The second vehicle is a dining car made in 1930 followed by a "Concertina" built in 1918. The leading vehicle was made in 1940 and the train ascends Honeybourne Bank up to Chipping Campden tunnel behind No. 7005 **Lamphey Castle** (later named **Sir Edward Elgar**) with a Worcester-Paddington express. This picture conveys the feelings mentioned in the preface. **27 August 1954**

A County 4-6-0 at speed with the through train from Margate to Birkenhead and about to go under the S.M.J.R. near Fenny Compton. No. 1024 **County of Pembroke** is in charge with a bow-ended third behind the tender and Collet 7′ 0″ bogies.   **18 December 1954**

Deputising for the usual King, No. 5088 "Llanthony Abbey" has just passed Hatton station with the midday express from Birmingham to Paddington.   **18 January 1955**

Another view of the same train half way down Hatton Bank this time with No. 6020 **King Henry IV** in charge.   **19 January 1955**

ton Bank with a down freight for the Black Country. Beyond the snow covered field is the maintenance workshop of the Grand Union Canal and in the distance can be seen the smoking chimney of Hatton Hospital.
19 January 1955

The old London-Birmingham line of the G.W.R. is shown in the foreground as 2-6-2T No. 6102 takes the auto train up the bank towards Ardley and Bicester. The girder bridge shadowed at the top of the picture carries the down line over the old route and forms the Aynho flyover. **18 December 1954**

Two moguls meet by the S.M.J.R. over-bridge between Banbury and Leamington. No. 9314 with window cab is on the down line and No. 6321 comes into view from under the bridge. Both engines appear to have steam to spare.
18 December 1954

Chicheley Hall on the down main line at Hatton North Junction with a short freight, the second wagon being sheeted probably due to a leaky roof, certainly needed on this wet day. The line to Stratford-on-Avon branches off to the right. This train was followed by "Coronation" class 4-6-2 No. 46327 **City of Bristol** on the 09.10 Paddington-Birkenhead undergoing trials on the Western Region.   **27 April 1955**

No. **4900 Saint Martin** was the prototype of the Hall class, rebuilt from Saint class No. 2925 in 1924 but with 6′ 0″ coupled wheels. The local train from Leamington to Worcester via Stratford-on-Avon is passing the cold storage plant near Warwick and the signal box was a World War II building. The mile post gives the distance from Paddington via Oxford.   **30 April 1955**

R.O.D. No. 3038 toils up the loop past Budbrooke Box on Hatton Bank with a 2-6-2T pushing up at the rear. **30 April 1955**

In unlined black livery 2-6-2T No. 4112 has a local train from Birmingham to Leamington passing over Rowington troughs (usually known as ''Lapworth'' troughs). The water storage tank is on the right. **30 April 1955**

Still retaining its streamlined cab this was the King fitted with partial streamlining in 1935. The bullnose prevented reporting numbers being carried on the smokebox and No. 6014 **King Henry VII** carried these on top of the buffer beam. In this picture the 09.00 Birmingham-Paddington rounds the curve travelling very fast at the foot of Hatton Bank. **7 May 1955**

With a good showing of Hawkesworth stock No. 1024 **County of Pembroke** picks up water on "Lapworth" troughs with the Margate-Birkenhead through train.
30 April 1955

Fruit vans from the Vale of Evesham are attached to this auto train shown heading towards Broadway shortly after leaving Honeybourne. The engine is 0-4-2T No. 1406 and you can see the Cotswold hills in the background.
7 May 1955

Rounding the curve past Norton Junction station No. 5081 **Lockheed Hudson** is in charge of the midday train from Worcester to Paddington complete with 70′ diner. The engine, one of twelve renamed after World War II aircraft in 1940-1, is in a state of cleanliness typical of the Castles at Worcester shed. **7 May 1955**

A blast of steam from the whistle announces the approach of the evening Worcester-Paddington train to Evesham station. To the left can be seen the shed and Midland line bearing off to Ashchurch.

7 May 1955

No. 7029 **Clun Castle** nears Honeybourne Junction and is about to pass under the Worcester-Paddington main line with a West Country returning holiday express to Wolverhampton. Shedded at Newton Abbot the engine will probably return the next day on the Sunday "Cornishman". Note the fine G.W.R. signals with long arms erected around the time of the First World War.

7 May 1955

The evening parcels train coasts down the bank a mile from Leamington. The down trains come into sight through the trees at the left edge of the picture and travel down the embankment just visible above the first coach. Chesterton Windmill now so beautifully restored can be seen on the skyline above the whistles

Is this not a unique combination of King and Star? Climbing Hatton Bank No. 6006 **King George I** and No. 4061 **Glastonbury Abbey** with the 14.10 Paddington-Birkenhead. This sight was expected as the Star worked the first part of the 09.00 Birmingham-Paddington in the morning and the King took the main train, thus there were two engines available for the return working.   **18 June 1955**

Instead of a "Stag Party" the evening before I was married the perfect form of relaxation was to sit by the line and watch the trains go by. In this case it is 2-6-0 No. 6376 with a local train from Chester to Birkenhead approaching Bromborough on a fine summer evening.   **24 June 1955**

Working the 17.10 Paddington-Wolverhampton, No. 6011 **King James I** with steam shut off approaches Leamington. The engine shedded at Wolverhampton Stafford Road worked up to London on the midday train from Birmingham.   **25 July 1955**

The down distant signal stands guard near Leamington as No. 5015 **Kingswear Castle** passes with the "Inter-City", at that time worked by a Wolverhampton engine.
2 September 1955

No. 7822 **Foxcote Manor** and 2-6-0 No. 6345 have just departed from Chester station with Midland Region stock and are about to cross over to the up slow line which will take them onto the Western at Saltney Junction. The mogul is fresh from overhaul at Swindon and note the L.N.W.R. signal box straddling the track.
3 September 1955

A vacuum fitted freight by-passes Chester station using the Northwest part of the triangle. 2-8-0 No. 3827 has come from Birkenhead and heads south to Shrewsbury.
3 September 1955

Two views of No. 4061 **Glastonbury Abbey** at Tyseley Shed the evening before working a Stephenson Locomotive Society special to Swindon. Note the heater for frost prevention underneath the water column and the arm with cranked elbow which was necessary on the introduction of the 4000 gallon tenders.
10 September 1955

Halls under repair at Swindon works. In the centre No. 6997 **Bryn-Ivor Hall**, and on the right showing its super heater elements is No. 5917 **Westminster Hall**. Various parts can be seen on the floor including blast pipe, cylinder covers and a chimney over on the left of the picture.
11 September 1955

The first double chimney King being towed out of Swindon shed by 2-6-2T No. 5536 for photographs to be taken, although ash dust appears to cover the rear coupled wheels. You will notice the grit being put on the rails to stop wheel spin on the tank engine which was in great difficulty. No. 6015 **King Richard III** also has a self-cleaning smokebox. **11 September 1955**

Outside Swindon works No. 6000 **King George V** stands cold after overhaul. This picture shows the ugly final form of single chimney which fortunately was only fitted to a few of the Kings.
11 September 1955

L.S.W.R. 4-4-0 No. 30304 Class T.9. has just arrived at Welshpool with the Talyllyn Railway Preservation Society Special from Paddington to Towyn. Dukedog No. 9027 awaits a shunting operation before helping the train over the old Cambrian main line.

T.R.P.S. Special now with the Dukedog inside the T.9. leaves Welshpool station. Shrewsbury shed cleaned the T.9. and painted the buffers white. **24 September 1955**

No. 5010 **Restormel Castle** was one of the first Castles to be withdrawn apart from ''rebuilds'' from Stars which except for 4037 were scrapped earlier. This picture was taken about four years prior to this date showing it hurrying the Wolverhampton-Weymouth express past Hatton North signal box. **5 November 1955**

Ex-works in black livery 2-8-0 No. 2841 comes through Leamington Spa on the down fast line with a freight for the north. The point rodding has wooden covers on its full length as many of the passenger trains had their wheels tapped at Leamington, and this enabled the staff to walk safely. **21 November 1955**

The G.W.R. football specials from London to Birmingham climbs Hatton Bank with an Old Oak Common Castle No. 7030 **Cranbrook Castle** at the head.
17 March 1956

No. 5090 **Neath Abbey** approaches Chipping Campden station with a late morning express from Worcester to Paddington. The wooden gantry on the left protects the telegraph wires from the power lines crossing the picture should they be brought down. **3 April 1956**

Later in the afternoon with a strong north-west wind blowing, the exhaust from No. 5037 **Monmouth Castle** follows the engine as it climbs slowly up the bank to Chipping Campden tunnel with a train from Worcester to Paddington. **3 April 1956**

Two months after fitting with the early straight sided double chimney, No. 6001 **King Edward VII** passes Warwick station with the 10.00 Birmingham-Paddington. This engine was the first double chimney King to be received by Wolverhampton Stafford Road shed

Cup Final day must have had a Midland club playing at Wembley as No. 5912 **Queen's Hall** comes through Leamington on the up fast line with coloured ribbon between the lamps on the buffer beam. No. 6861 **Crynant Grange** stands in the up platform waiting to

Still with G.W.R. on the tender side eight years after nationalisation, 2-8-0 No. 2848 coasts towards Leamington with a down freight. The fireman concentrates on looking out for the down distant signal as the safety valves pour unwanted steam into the warm

2-6-2T No. 4124 has just left Parkgate station with a local train from West Kirby to Hooton. This part of the line now taken up is planted with shrubs and as a footpath is part of the "Wirral Way". **2 August 1956**

A toolbox for P.W. tools and a platelayer's hut stand on either side of the main line as No. 7034 **Ince Castle** comes up the grade towards Box Tunnel with the 08.20 Weston-super-Mare—Paddington express. A North Eastern coach leads the B.R. coaching stock on this dull August morning.

Shooting out of the west portal of Box Tunnel is No. 5093 **Upton Castle** with the down "Bristolian". **3 August 1956**

2-8-0 No. 2843 starts the descent from Whiteball Tunnel towards Exeter with a freight. The banker can be seen standing beyond the bridge in the background after helping the train from Taunton. **3 August 1956**

On the final 1 in 37 of the climb to Dainton Tunnel, No. 1006 **County of Cornwall** and No. 4091 **Dudley Castle** have steam to spare before the equally precipitous descent the other side to Newton Abbot. Above the cab of the Castle can be seen a mirror to enable the signalman to see the tail lamps of up trains when the view is blocked by a down train passing through the tunnel. **4 August 1956**

Round the curve from Aller Junction comes No. 4077 **Chepstow Castle** with an express for Plymouth. The main road from Newton Abbot to Torquay runs along in front of the wood above the Torquay branch. 2-8-0 No. 2843 waits in the loop for a banker to come up behind for the slog up to Dainton Tunnel.

3 August 1956

The sighting board shows up the signal arm position of the up distant for Aller Junction in the background as No. 7813 **Freshford Manor** and No. 5918 **Walton Hall** lift their load up the early stages of Dainton towards Stoneycombe quarry. A rather restricted railway allotment is well cared for on the left of the picture.

4 August 1956

No. 4900 **Saint Martin** appears to be doing all the work with No. 6004 **King George III** following gently behind, but the roar of the exhaust from both engines proved otherwise. The Hall class engine would come off at Newton Abbot. **4 August 1956**

No. 6802 **Bampton Grange** and No. 6021 **King Richard II** are on the final straight up to Dainton Tunnel with 09.20 St. Ives-Paddington.
4 August 1956

are level on the right of the picture and the mirror previously mentioned shows up well above the seventh coach.
No. **6996 Blackwell Hall** and No. **5967 Bickmarsh Hall** have a holiday extra for the west.
4 August 1956

A fourteen coach load, composed mainly of Midland region stock, comprises the 07.30 Penzance-Liverpool about to pass under the A381 Newton Abbot-Totnes road on the climb up to Dainton Summit behind No. 4950 **Patshull Hall** and No. 4056 **Princess Margaret**. This was the

With steam shut off, B.R. class 4 No. 75026 and No. 6026 **King John** descend the 1 in 65 of Rattery Bank with the 12.30 Newquay-Paddington. Note the spring loaded catch points on the down line adjacent to the King and the bird which has been disturbed by the train. **4 August 1956**

Skirting the outskirts of Plymouth, No. 6931 **Aldborough Hall** heads west with what I believe to be the Cornish Riviera Limited. The L.S.W.R. main line to Waterloo via Exeter is shown in the foreground guarded by a typical lattice girder signal. **5 August 1956**

at Newton Abbot and was usually replaced by two Halls. The King would then wait for the 10.35 from Paddington, which was also King hauled, and the two would then double head the train onto Plymouth for a further engine change. This photograph shows No. 6025 **King Henry III** and No. 6019 **King Henry V** with the 10.35 Paddington-Penzance starting the climb to Wrangaton shortly after passing through Totnes. The headboard should of course have been removed.   **4 August 1956**

At the foot of Hemerdon Bank
No. 7814 **Fringford Manor** and No. 7909 **Heveningham Hall** round the curve and into Plympton station at the start of Hemerdon Bank. The black dots in the sky are birds looking for some lift as they circle on a hot summer day.   **5 August 1956**

Half-way up Hemerdon Bank
No. 7820 **Dinmore Manor** and No. 5943 **Elmdon Hall** are hard at work with a holiday train for the North West. Both drivers appear relaxed and are enjoying having their photographs taken.   **6 August 1956**

Approaching the Summit of Hemerdon Bank
The outskirts of Plymouth may be seen above the top of the bridge as No. 5098 **Clifford Castle** and No. 6839 **Hewell Grange** come off the 1 in 75 final stages of the climb to Hemerdon siding with another holiday train for the Midland region.   **5 August 1956**

On the 1 in 42 bank of Hemerdon No. 1006 **County of Cornwall** has an excursion train for Goodrington Sands as it blackens the sky and shatters the peace of the woods on either side of the line. **6 August 1956**

This well known spot for picture taking is deserted early in the morning as the sun climbs into the clear sky, casting dense shadows against the cliff from the exhaust of 2-8-0 No. 3834 with an up freight passing through Teignmouth station. The two brick pillars of the bridge used to straddle the broad gauge tracks.
8 August 1956

A view well known in G.W.R. official publications looking east and taken from the road bridge crossing the estuary of the River Teign. No. 5992 **Horton Hall** has a down train on a scorching hot summer day when all the carriage windows are wide open and with the passengers hoping for the weather to continue like this for the next two weeks. **8 August 1956**

Even in the days of steam I did not photograph everything which came along and, although this train could be heard down at Aller Junction, I did not load the shutter on the camera until the black smoke was visible over the trees. No. 6957 **Northcliffe Hall** and No. 6026 **King John** struggle up the 1 in 41 of Dainton Bank with a Paddington-Penzance express probably leaving London at 11.30. **8 August 1956**

Brakes hard on as the 12.30 Penzance to Kensington Milk train has just passed Stoneycombe Quarry and descends rapidly down Dainton to Aller Junction. No. 6000 **King George V** with slotted bogie frame leads No. 6869 **Resolven Grange** on their way to London, dropping off the gas tanks (at the rear of the train) at Swindon for refilling. **8 August 1956**

The 08.00 Plymouth-Crewe has just passed through Dawlish station with an immaculate No. 1017 **County of Hereford** returning to its home shed at Shrewsbury. The train carried through carriages to Liverpool and Glasgow. **9 August 1956**

The Great Western enthusiasts who proclaim the merits of their locomotives and say that they never produced dramatic smoke effects to show up any boiler design inefficiencies, may care to study these two photographs. No. 1015 **County of Gloucester** with ten coaches returns to Plymouth from Goodrington Sands with a day excursion. The location is the final few yards of the approach to Dainton Tunnel where the gradient is 1 in 44 and the train will be travelling at running pace. The smoke hangs in the cutting down below in the woods on a summer evening when there is a flat calm and the shadow creeps slowly up the field on the right.

8 August 1956

No. 6003 **King George III** speeds the Cornish Riviera Limited along the sea wall between Dawlish and Dawlish Warren with the up train. What a magnificent place it is to watch the trains go by as one wanders along the sea walk for a gentle stroll. The fireman is hard at work getting the fire ready for the climb to Whiteball beyond Exeter and the engine has the final form of a single chimney.   **9 August 1956**

A view from the top of Langstone Rock looking south west with Dawlish in the background. No. 5028 **Llantilio Castle** has a 14-coach load of Great Western stock heading towards Exeter.   **9 August 1956**

Dawlish Warren station with the 09.30 Paddington-Falmouth passing through behind No. 70016 **Ariel** and No. 5098 **Clifford Castle.** Whilst the fashion in clothes may not change very much look at the collection of ancient "air polluters" in the car park. **9 August 1956**

The annual special organised by the Midland Area of the Stephenson Locomotive Society again heads towards Swindon for a visit to the Works and shed. After visiting Hereford Barton shed, part of which is shown on the left, No. 4056 **Princess Margaret**, cleaned at Tyseley shed and with transfers on the buffer beam, accelerates into a dull and wet day.
9 September 1956

On the double track section of the Cambrian main line, Wainwright class D. 4-4-0 No. 31075 and Dean Goods 0-6-0 No. 2538 have just passed through Newtown with the Talyllyn Railway Preservation Society Special from London to Towyn. The inspector and fireman appear to be having trouble in making the injector pick up. In the lower photograph the pair with their five coach load have crossed the Welsh hills and are on the descent to Machynlleth with a steady drizzle setting in.
22 September 1956